EXPLORE THE UNITED STATES

# SOUTH DAKOTA

Sarah Tieck

**Big Buddy Books**

An Imprint of Abdo Publishing
abdobooks.com

# abdobooks.com

Published by Abdo Publishing, a division of ABDO, PO Box 398166, Minneapolis, Minnesota 55439. Copyright © 2020 by Abdo Consulting Group, Inc. International copyrights reserved in all countries. No part of this book may be reproduced in any form without written permission from the publisher. Big Buddy Books™ is a trademark and logo of Abdo Publishing.

Printed in the United States of America, North Mankato, Minnesota
102019
012020

 THIS BOOK CONTAINS RECYCLED MATERIALS

Design: Aruna Rangarajan, Mighty Media, Inc.
Production: Mighty Media, Inc.
Editor: Jessica Rusick

Cover Photograph: Shutterstock Images
Interior Photographs: Alamy Photo, p. 20; AP Images, p. 27 (top left); Danita Delimont/Alamy Photo, p. 29 (top right); DenisTangneyJr/iStockphoto, p. 9 (bottom left); James Nord/AP Images, p. 27 (top right); Jim Mone/AP Images, p. 27; Liliboas/iStockphoto, p. 30 (middle); RICHARD DREW/AP Images, p. 23; Shutterstock Images, pp. 4, 5, 6, 7, 9, 10, 11, 13, 15, 17, 19, 21, 22, 24, 25, 26, 28, 29, 30; Wikimedia Commons, p. 26 (bottom)

Populations figures from census.gov

Library of Congress Control Number: 2019943192

**Publisher's Cataloging-in-Publication Data**
Names: Tieck, Sarah, author.
Title: South Dakota / by Sarah Tieck
Description: Minneapolis, Minnesota : Abdo Publishing, 2020 | Series: Explore the United States | Includes online resources and index.
Identifiers: ISBN 9781532191459 (lib. bdg.) | ISBN 9781532178184 (ebook)
Subjects: LCSH: U.S. states--Juvenile literature. | Midwest States--Juvenile literature. | Physical geography--United States--Juvenile literature. | South Dakota--History--Juvenile literature.
Classification: DDC 978.3--dc23

# CONTENTS

# CHAPTER 1
# ONE NATION

The United States is a diverse country. It has farmland, cities, coasts, and mountains. Its people come from many different backgrounds. And, its history covers more than 200 years.

Today the country includes 50 states. South Dakota is one of these states. Let's learn more about this state and its story!

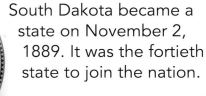

**DID YOU KNOW?**

South Dakota became a state on November 2, 1889. It was the fortieth state to join the nation.

Custer State Park is one of the state's natural wonders.

# CHAPTER 2

# SOUTH DAKOTA UP CLOSE

The United States has four main regions. South Dakota is in the Midwest.

South Dakota shares its borders with six other states. North Dakota is north. Minnesota and Iowa are east. Nebraska is south. Wyoming and Montana are west.

South Dakota has a total area of 77,116 square miles (199,730 sq km). About 882,000 people live there.

**DID YOU KNOW?**

Washington, DC, is the US capital city. Puerto Rico is a US commonwealth. This means it is governed by its own people.

Puerto Rico became a US commonwealth in 1952.

# ★ Regions of ★
# the United States

West
Midwest
South
Northeast

CANADA

WASHINGTON
MONTANA
NORTH DAKOTA
MICHIGAN
NEW HAMPSHIRE
VERMONT
MAINE
OREGON
IDAHO
SOUTH DAKOTA
MINNESOTA
WISCONSIN
PENNSYLVANIA
NEW YORK
MASSACHUSETTS
RHODE ISLAND
WYOMING
CONNECTICUT
CALIFORNIA
NEVADA
UTAH
COLORADO
NEBRASKA
IOWA
ILLINOIS
INDIANA
OHIO
NEW JERSEY
DELAWARE
MARYLAND
KANSAS
MISSOURI
KENTUCKY
WASHINGTON, DC
WEST VIRGINIA
ARIZONA
NEW MEXICO
OKLAHOMA
ARKANSAS
TENNESSEE
NORTH CAROLINA
VIRGINIA
SOUTH CAROLINA
PACIFIC OCEAN
ALABAMA
GEORGIA
TEXAS
MEXICO
MISSISSIPPI
FLORIDA
ATLANTIC OCEAN
LOUISIANA
Gulf of Mexico
ALASKA
HAWAII
PUERTO RICO

N
W E
S

# CHAPTER 3

# IMPORTANT CITIES

Pierre (PIHR) is South Dakota's capital. It has 13,980 people. It is located along the Missouri River. Historic Fort Pierre is nearby.

Sioux (SOO) Falls is the largest city in the state. It is home to 181,883 people. This city is on the Big Sioux River. It was named for the river's large waterfall.

PIERRE South Dakota's capitol was completed in 1910.

ABERDEEN is named after Aberdeen, Scotland.

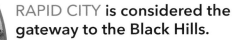

RAPID CITY is considered the gateway to the Black Hills.

SIOUX FALLS holds Falls Park, a tourist attraction where the Big Sioux River flows over rocks.

The second-largest city in South Dakota is Rapid City. It has 75,443 people. The city is near the Black Hills and Mount Rushmore. Many people vacation there.

Aberdeen is South Dakota's third-largest city, with 28,562 people. It has a historic Main Street. The city is home to Wylie Park, where people can bike, picnic, and mini golf.

Pinkish-brown rock surrounds the falls of the Big Sioux River. This type of rock was used for buildings in the Sioux Falls area.

13

# CHAPTER 4

# SOUTH DAKOTA IN HISTORY

South Dakota's history includes Native Americans and explorers. Native Americans lived on the land for thousands of years before others arrived. Many hunted bison. Others grew crops.

In 1682, French explorers claimed what is now South Dakota. In 1803, the United States bought much of this land as part of the Louisiana Purchase. After years as a US territory, South Dakota became a state in 1889.

In 1874, gold was discovered in the Black Hills. As more gold was found, mining towns, such as Deadwood, were created.

# CHAPTER 5

# ACROSS THE LAND

South Dakota has thick forests, low mountains, grassy plains, caves, rivers, and lakes. Major rivers include the Missouri and the Big Sioux. The Black Hills and the Badlands are in western South Dakota.

Many types of animals make their homes in this state. These include white-tailed deer, pronghorns, and ring-necked pheasants. Many fish including walleye, perch, and bass swim in the state's waters.

**DID YOU KNOW?**

In July, the average high temperature in South Dakota is 85°F (29°C). In January, it is 30°F (-1°C).

The Badlands are known for unusual rock formations. They have been shaped by wind and water over many years.

# CHAPTER 6

# EARNING A LIVING

South Dakota has many important businesses. People work in banks, schools, and hospitals. The state is one of the country's most popular vacation spots. So, a lot of people have jobs helping visitors.

South Dakota has many natural resources. Its mines provide gold, sand, and stone. Farms cover much of the land. Wheat, soybeans, sunflowers, and corn are major crops.

South Dakota is the nation's number-one producer of bison.

# CHAPTER 7

# NATURAL WONDER

The Black Hills National Forest is in southwestern South Dakota and part of Wyoming. This is a popular vacation spot. It is famous for its rock cliffs, pine forests, and grassy plains.

For many years, Native Americans lived in this area. After gold was found in 1874, settlers arrived. In 1897, President Grover Cleveland set aside this land. It became the Black Hills National Forest in 1907. Today, people camp, hike, and ride motorcycles there.

**DID YOU KNOW?**

The Black Hills look dark from a distance. That is how they got their name.

Black Elk Peak is in the Black Hills. It is the state's highest point, at 7,242 feet (2,207 m). Visitors can climb Harney Peak for a great view of Black Hills National Forest.

# CHAPTER 8

# HOMETOWN HEROES

Many famous people have lived in South Dakota. Laura Ingalls Wilder was born in Pepin, Wisconsin, in 1867. Her family claimed a homestead in De Smet in 1880.

Wilder wrote novels about her family's life. She became known for books such as *Little House on the Prairie*. Wilder wrote *By the Shores of Silver Lake*, *The Long Winter*, and *Little Town on the Prairie* about South Dakota.

**DID YOU KNOW?**
Wilder's first book came out in 1932.

In De Smet, visitors can see many of the sites mentioned in Wilder's books.

Tom Brokaw was born in Webster in 1940. He is a famous television reporter. He led NBC Nightly News from 1982 to 2004. In 2014, he received the Presidential Medal of Freedom.

Brokaw is also an author of several books. In 2002, he wrote *A Long Way from Home*. It is about growing up in South Dakota.

**DID YOU KNOW?**

Brokaw attended the University of South Dakota in Vermillion. He worked at radio stations in the area.

Brokaw became known for reporting news in a calm, clear way.

# CHAPTER 9

# A GREAT STATE

The story of South Dakota is important to the United States. The people and places that make up this state offer something special to the country. Together with all the states, South Dakota helps make the United States great.

The Missouri River forms part of South Dakota's border with Nebraska. The Gavins Point Dam is located on this border.

South Dakota is known for Mount Rushmore. The faces of four presidents are carved into this famous cliff. They are George Washington, Thomas Jefferson, Theodore Roosevelt, and Abraham Lincoln.

# TIMELINE

**1889**

The Dakota Territory became two states on November 2. North Dakota was the thirty-ninth state. South Dakota was the fortieth state.

**1804**

Meriwether Lewis and William Clark began to explore what is now South Dakota.

**1800s**

President Thomas Jefferson arranged for the United States to buy land in the **Louisiana Purchase**. It included most of present-day South Dakota.

**1803**

Congress created the Dakota Territory.

**1861**

After years of fighting over land, US soldiers killed hundreds of Native Americans near Wounded Knee Creek.

**1890**

**1973**

Native Americans held a **protest** for 71 days at Wounded Knee. They did this to get better treatment from the US government.

**2019**

Kristi Noem became the state's first female governor.

**1927**

Work started on Mount Rushmore.

1900s

2000s

Four dams on the Missouri River were completed to provide power to South Dakota.

**1966**

Heavy snowfall caused historic spring flooding in South Dakota. This destroyed homes and roads.

**2011**

# TOUR BOOK

Do you want to go to South Dakota? If you visit the state, here are some places to go and things to do!

**SEE**

Walk around the Corn Palace in Mitchell. This famous building features art made of corn, grains, and grasses. The first Corn Palace was built in 1892.

**PLAY**

Spend time in the Black Hills. Look for wild animals, such as bison. And, stop for trail hikes.

While you're there, swim in the cool waters of Sylvan Lake.

## EXPLORE

See herds of wild horses in the Black Hills Wild Horse Sanctuary.

The grounds also have old frontier homes and Native American drawings called petroglyphs (PEH-truh-glihfs).

## REMEMBER

Visit the old mining town of Deadwood. There, you can see what life was like during South Dakota's gold rush.

## DISCOVER

Explore underground at Jewel Cave or Wind Cave (*pictured*). Both are among the world's longest cave systems!

# FAST FACTS

▶ STATE FLOWER

American
Pasqueflower

▶ STATE TREE

Black Hills
Spruce

▶ STATE BIRD

Ring-Necked
Pheasant

▶ STATE FLAG:

▶ NICKNAME:
Mount Rushmore State

▶ DATE OF STATEHOOD:
November 2, 1889

▶ POPULATION (RANK):
882,235
(46th most-populated state)

▶ TOTAL AREA (RANK):
77,116 square miles
(17th largest state)

▶ STATE CAPITAL:
Pierre

▶ POSTAL ABBREVIATION:
SD

▶ MOTTO:
"Under God the People Rule"

# GLOSSARY

**capital**—a city where government leaders meet.

**diverse**—made up of things that are different from each other.

**fort**—a building with strong walls to guard against enemies.

**homestead**—a piece of land given to settlers by the US government.

**Louisiana Purchase**—land the United States purchased from France in 1803. It extended from the Mississippi River to the Rocky Mountains and from Canada through the Gulf of Mexico.

**plains**—flat or rolling land without trees.

**protest**—an event where people speak out against or object to something.

**region**—a large part of a country that is different from other parts.

**resource**—a supply of something useful or valued.

# ONLINE RESOURCES

**Booklinks**
**NONFICTION NETWORK**
FREE! ONLINE NONFICTION RESOURCES

To learn more about South Dakota, please visit **abdobooklinks.com** or scan this QR code. These links are routinely monitored and updated to provide the most current information available.

# INDEX